I0616235

FREQUENCY JUSTICE

The Power of Compassion, Safety, and Joy

NICHOLE SLOAN

To request permissions, contact the publisher at
compassionbasedrecovery@gmail.com

Paperback: 979-8-218-86341-8
Ebook: 979-8-218-86344-9

First paperback edition October 2025

Written & Edited by Nichole Sloan
Layout by Henrietta Sampson

Printed by Compassion Based Recovery in the USA.

CompassionBasedRecovery.com

Acknowledgment of Authorship

This book was written and created by Nichole Sloan, grounded
in her clinical experience, personal healing, and frequency-
based framework. Some organizational and editorial support
was provided using AI tools under her creative direction. All
protocols, insights, and teachings remain her original work.

Author's Note

This book was written in partnership with wisdom greater than my own. The words came through me, but they do not belong only to me. They carry the resonance of teachers seen and unseen, woven through lifetimes and lineages.

What you will read here is not meant to be doctrine, but invitation. It is a remembering of truths that live within all of us: compassion, safety, and joy are not luxuries, but the most powerful frequencies we can choose.

I offer this book as both student and steward, with gratitude for the guidance that has walked beside me, and with deep reverence for you, the reader, who carries the next thread of this work forward.

May these teachings benefit all beings.

May this offering reach those who are ready to remember.

Contents

"Humankind has not woven the web of life. We are but one thread within it. Whatever we do to the web, we do to ourselves. All things are bound together. All things connect."

Chief Seattle

Introduction

The Pulse of Frequency Justice

There are times in history when the world trembles at the edge of collapse. Fear grows loud, greed spreads like fire, and distortion tries to convince us that suffering is inevitable. But in every age, there are those who quietly carry another vibration. People who return again and again to compassion, even when anger is easier. People who choose to create safety, even when the world feels dangerous. People who reclaim joy, even in the face of despair. This is what I call frequency justice.

Frequency justice is a theoretical offering bridging both science and spirituality. It is not a law passed in a courtroom, or a policy written on paper. It is a lived act of defiance.

Frequency justice is choosing compassion when the world teaches cruelty. It is offering safety in the midst of chaos. It is daring to laugh, love, and savor beauty in a system that profits from despair. We may not be able to topple systems overnight, but we can create coherence within ourselves and our communities. This is how frequency justice becomes embodied.

We are deeply interconnected to one another both in the physical and the non-physical planes of reality. In this book we explore how our personal expressions of compassion, safety and joy effect the nature and structure of our shared reality from a metaphysical, spiritual and scientific lens.

The language I use throughout this book draws from several disciplines that all describe patterns, structures, and inter- actions in different ways. I reference quantum language as it provides an accessible model, while my clinical work, contemplative practice, and lived spiritual experience sug- gest that similar patterns may exist in the subtle emotional and energetic architecture of human connection.

Within this framework, we will explore how each of our choices creates a pulse—an imprint of coherence in the collective field. When enough pulses converge, they weave nodes of crystalline stability into the inter-connected lattice of the world. These concepts are not abstract. They are the reason a person can walk into a space and suddenly feel calmer, safer, more alive.

The truth is, you are already contributing to this collective field, whether you realize it or not. Every breath softened, every kind word offered, every act of care ripples farther than you can see. This book is an invitation to remember your role in this great weaving. To understand that your daily choices are not small, they are the architecture of collective liberation. And to realize that the coherence you cultivate in yourself becomes medicine not only for yourself and the planet but for generations to come.

We may not always be able to stop wars, topple unjust systems, or erase centuries of pain overnight. But we can anchor a vibration that refuses to collapse. We can live as proof that compassion, safety, and joy are stronger than distortion. And together, our nodes of coherence become the seeds of a world reborn.

Welcome to Frequency Justice. You have always been part of it. This is simply your reminder.

"We are the ones we
have been waiting for."

June Jordan

Chapter 1

The Call to Frequency Justice

The world feels heavy right now. Fear echoes through our newsfeeds. Division grows louder in politics and in neighborhoods. Many people feel caught in the cycle of anger, despair, and helplessness. I've felt it, too.

I call this distortion—the vibration of fear, greed, hatred, and despair that pulls us away from our wholeness. Distortion convinces us that cruelty is normal, that safety is impossible, and that joy is a luxury. It feeds on our nervous systems until we forget that another way is possible.

But frequency justice is that other way.

What Frequency Justice Means

Frequency justice is the deliberate act of choosing compassion, safety, and joy as a counterforce to distortion. It's not about ignoring pain or pretending everything is fine. It's about holding pain differently—*transforming it* instead of transmitting it.

- When I choose compassion, I interrupt the cycle of cruelty.

- When I create safety, I build ground where fear cannot root.

- When I reclaim joy, I declare that despair cannot win.

These choices may seem small, but they ripple far beyond the moment. Each act becomes a pulse of coherence in the collective. Each pulse joins others to form a stabilizing lattice that holds us steady in turbulent times.

Why It Matters Now

Distortion thrives on despair. When enough people give up hope, systems of oppression tighten their grip. But coherence spreads just as powerfully. Neuroscience tells us our emotions ripple through groups—we regulate one another constantly. Spirit tells us compassion, safety, and joy are not just feelings, but Source-coded frequencies. They can't be erased; they can only be forgotten.

Every time you return to these frequencies, you help the world remember.

Your Role in the Lattice

Most people build the lattice unconsciously. They create nodes through kindness, connection, and care without naming them. But intentional acts magnify the effect. When you deliberately choose compassion, when you intentionally soften your nervous system, when you reclaim joy against despair—you strengthen the lattice for all beings.

Coherence is liberation. When your system is steady, you make space for others to breathe. When communities anchor safety, they create the conditions for freedom. Frequency justice is how we begin to rebuild—not from the top down, but from the inside out.

A First Invitation

You don't have to do this perfectly. You don't have to become enlightened overnight. Frequency justice is not about erasing your humanity—it's about returning to compassion even when you shake, choosing safety even when you feel afraid, and daring joy even when despair whispers loudly.

Here is your first practice:

- Pause once today.

- Place your hand on your heart.

- Whisper: "May compassion flow through me, for myself and for others."

Notice what shifts, even slightly. That small act is already frequency justice.

"Compassion is the radicalism of our time."

H.H. Dalai Lama XIV

Chapter 2

Compassion as Shield & Seed

Compassion is the first current of frequency justice. It is both shield and seed: a shield against distortion, and a seed that grows coherence in the collective.

Distortion thrives on cruelty, division, and shame. Compassion interrupts that cycle. It says: I see your suffering, and I will not turn away. In that moment, distortion loses its grip, because compassion refuses to participate in its game.

But compassion is not only defense—it is also creation. Every time you choose to meet pain with softness, you plant a seed. That seed does not just stay in you. It ripples into your family, your community, your city, and into the lattice itself. Compassion is how we remember our interconnectedness. It is the first step toward collective liberation.

Compassion in the Nervous System

Compassion is not only an idea—it lives in the body. When we soften our gaze, slow our breath, or place a hand on our heart, we signal safety to our nervous system. Safety opens the door to compassion. Fear and compassion cannot take root in the same soil; you cannot both attack and extend care in the same heartbeat.

That's why compassion practices are so powerful: they interrupt the body's survival loops and create new pathways of presence. From a clinical lens, compassion reshapes the brain's appraisal system, reducing reactivity and strengthening resilience. From a spiritual lens, compassion opens the channel of Source, allowing love to flow through us.

Scientific Insight:

Modern research confirms what the lattice has always held true: compassion is not only morally powerful, but also biologically powerful.

- Compassion lowers stress and worry. Studies consistently show that people who practice compassion-focused exercises experience less anxiety, depression, and inner criticism.

- Compassion changes the body. When someone practices compassion, the heart rhythm slows and steadies, breathing deepens, and the nervous system shifts into balance. This creates resilience and calm, even under pressure.

- Compassion reshapes the brain. Brain imaging shows that compassion activates regions tied to empathy, joy, and prosocial motivation. Over time, these areas strengthen, making compassion more natural and automatic.

- Compassion strengthens relationships. People who practice compassion feel more connected to others and tend to act with greater kindness. This ripple effect doesn't stop with one person—it spreads through families, communities, and networks.

- Compassion boosts well-being. With self-compassion especially, people report more confidence, more hope, and a greater ability to face difficulties without collapsing into despair.

Practicing Compassion in Daily Life

Compassion does not require grand gestures. It begins with how you speak to yourself in the quiet moments of your day.

- When you notice your own anxiety: "May I be gentle with myself right now."

- When you see another's suffering: "May you know peace. May you know ease."

- When the world feels overwhelming: "May compassion hold us all."

These simple phrases soften your nervous system and ripple outward. They do not erase pain, but they change the field in which pain lives.

Compassion as Collective Medicine

Think of compassion like rain falling on scorched earth. Each drop may seem small, but over time, it transforms the landscape.

When compassion is practiced collectively, it becomes medicine for entire communities. It can shift conversations, interrupt violence, and restore dignity where it has been stripped away. You may not always see the result of your compassion, but the lattice carries it forward.

Compassionate Reflection & Practice

1. Recall a time when compassion changed the course of your day. What shifted?

2. Where can you offer compassion today—to yourself, to a loved one, or even to a stranger?

3. Practice the simple mantra: "May compassion flow through me, for myself and others."

Every repetition builds the shield. Every repetition plants the seed.

With compassion, you are not just comforting yourself or another—you are weaving threads of coherence into the planetary lattice. Each act of compassion becomes both shield and seed.

"There's something revolutionary about creating a space for people to lay down what burdens them".

Prentis Hemphill

Chapter 3

Safety as Grounds for Liberation

If compassion is the shield and seed of frequency justice, safety is the soil. Without safety, compassion cannot root, and joy cannot bloom. Safety is what makes liberation possible.

Safety is more than the absence of danger. In frequency justice, safety is an active vibration that signals to the nervous system: you can soften here, you can expand here, you can live here.

Distortion thrives on instability—systems of oppression keep people fearful and uncertain because fear weakens our coherence. When we feel unsafe, we close our hearts, tighten our bodies and lose access to compassion and joy. Safety is not just comfort; it is a radical ground for healing and justice.

True, embodied safety—breaks distortion. It gives us back choice, breath, and belonging. When safety is present, nodes can root, and the lattice can strengthen. Without safety, coherence cannot hold.

Safety in the Body

Safety begins with the nervous system. When the body feels safe, the mind can open, relationships can heal, and communities can grow strong.

- Physiological safety: Deep, easeful breath, a steady heart rhythm, the ability to rest and digest.

- Emotional safety: Knowing it is acceptable to feel, to cry, to be angry, and still be held.

- Relational safety: Trusting others not to harm, shame, or abandon.

From a clinical perspective, safety restores regulation to the autonomic nervous system. From a spiritual perspective, safety opens the root gate—the energetic foundation where survival fear is transmuted into trust.

Creating Safety for Yourself

Liberation work does not begin with grand revolutions; it begins with tending your own root system.

- Anchor the breath: Slow, steady inhales and long, gentle exhales.

- Ground into place: Sit with your back against a tree or feel your feet pressing into the earth.

- Self-talk as shelter: Speak to yourself the way a loving guardian would: "You are safe. You are here. You belong. You are worthy. You are loveable."

These practices build an inner refuge. You become less vulnerable to distortion when you carry safety within your own body.

Creating Safety for Others

Safety is contagious. Just as anxiety ripples through groups, so does steadiness.

- In therapy or caregiving: Your calm presence helps regulate others' nervous systems.

- In community spaces: Setting boundaries, showing consistency, and practicing non-judgment creates collective safety.

- In justice movements: Communities anchored in safety resist collapse when threatened by external pressure.

To create safety is not to coddle or avoid conflict—it is to ensure that even in conflict, dignity remains intact.

Safety as Justice

In a distorted world, safety is not neutral—it is liberation work. When you help someone feel safe, you interrupt systems that thrive on fear. When you claim safety for yourself, you refuse to let distortion define your existence.

Safety allows people to rest, to dream, to create, and to imagine new futures. Without safety, liberation is theory. With safety, liberation becomes possible.

Scientific Insight:

Research on trauma and stress has shown again and again that safety is not optional for healing—it is foundational.

- The nervous system is always scanning. Neuroscientists call this neuroception—the body's unconscious way of asking "Am I safe or not?" If the body senses danger, it shifts into fight, flight, or freeze.

- Safety calms the body. Environments and practices that promote safety—such as steady breathing, compassionate relationships, or calm spaces—activate the parasympathetic nervous system. This lowers heart rate and stress hormones, restoring balance.

- Safety builds resilience. Trauma research shows that when people feel safe enough, they can process difficult experiences without being overwhelmed. Safety doesn't erase pain, but it makes it survivable and transformable.

- Safety spreads. When one person feels safe, others nearby often feel it too. This is how safety becomes a social field, not just a personal state.

Compassionate Reflection & Practice

1. Where do I feel safest in my body right now?

2. Where do I feel unsafe? How might I soften that space?

3. Who around me needs a moment of safety today? What simple action could I take to offer it?

Try this practice:

· Inhale slowly, exhale longer.

· With each breath, whisper: "I am safe. We are safe. The ground holds us."

In frequency justice, safety is not passive—it is a liberatory act. Every time you create safety in yourself, you stabilize your own lattice. Every time you extend safety to another— through kindness, calm presence, or even the tone of your voice—you weave threads of coherence that ripple outward.

The science of nervous system regulation and the meta-physics of the lattice point to the same truth: safety is freedom. When bodies feel safe, they unlock creativity, compassion, and joy. They become capable of building nodes that endure.

CHAPTER 3

"Tomorrow belongs
to those of us
who conceive of
it as belonging to
everyone; who lend
the best of ourselves
to it, and with joy".

Audre Lorde

Chapter 4

Joy as Revolutionary Act

If compassion shields us and safety steadies us, joy is what lifts us. Joy is often misunderstood as frivolous, selfish, or naive in hard times. But in truth, joy is one of the most radical expressions of frequency justice.

Distortion wants us to be exhausted, afraid, and despairing. It wants us to forget what it feels like to be alive, playful, and free. To choose joy in the face of suffering is not denial—it is defiance. It is saying: "You cannot take my light, even here, even now."

Joy is not frivolous. In a world saturated with distortion, joy is an act of rebellion. To laugh, to dance, to savor beauty is to say: I refuse to let fear dictate the rhythm of my being.

In frequency justice, joy is not only personal—it is collective. Every spark of joy you allow becomes a radiant node in the lattice. Joy interrupts cycles of despair. It restores energy. It points toward the world that is still possible.

Joy in the Nervous System

From a physiological perspective, joy restores balance to the body. It shifts us out of fight-or-flight and into connection. It strengthens immune function, increases resilience, and restores our capacity to see possibility instead of only threat.

From a spiritual perspective, joy is a remembrance of Source. It is the vibration of wholeness breaking through distortion. Joy is a preview of liberation—an embodied taste of the world we are working toward.

Scientific Insight:

Positive psychology and well-being research affirm what the lattice has always known: joy is medicine.

- Joy boosts resilience. People who regularly experience positive emotions recover from stress more quickly and show stronger immunity.

- Joy rewires the brain. Practices that cultivate gratitude, awe, or delight increase activity in brain regions tied to reward and motivation, making it easier to access joy again in the future.

- Joy strengthens relationships. Shared joy builds bonds more deeply than shared struggle. Laughter and play are powerful tools of connection.

- Joy restores balance. Research shows that moments of joy can buffer the impact of trauma and chronic stress, giving people greater capacity to cope.

- Joy inspires action. Positive emotions broaden perspective and creativity, leading to more effective problem-solving and resilience in communities.

Everyday Joy as Resistance

Joy does not require extraordinary circumstances. It is found in small, ordinary moments that distortion cannot touch:

- The way sunlight scatters across your kitchen table.

- The laughter of a child.

- The quiet warmth of a pet sleeping against your body.

- A song that makes your whole spirit hum.

When you let yourself savor these moments, you reclaim ground from despair. Each spark of joy strengthens the lattice.

Collective Joy as Power

When communities come together in joy—through music, dance, celebration, ritual—they build resilience that oppression cannot erase. This is why joy has always been central to liberation movements: songs of freedom, gatherings of resistance, celebrations that defy fear.

Collective joy tells distortion: "We are unbreakable."

The Challenge of Joy

For many, joy feels harder to access than compassion or safety. Trauma, loss, and oppression make joy feel unsafe, or even impossible. This is why reclaiming joy is an act of courage.

- Permission: Allow yourself to enjoy yourself without guilt, even when the world is suffering.

- Practice: Seek small moments, not grand experiences. Joy builds through consistency.

- Protection: Joy may trigger envy or dismissal in others. Protect your joy—it is sacred.

Compassionate Reflection & Practice

1. When was the last time you felt pure joy? What did it feel like in your body?

2. What small joy can you invite into today?

3. Try this practice:

   - Place your hands on your heart.

   - Recall one moment of delight from your life.

   - Breathe it in as though you are reliving it now.

   - Whisper: "Joy is not a luxury—it is my power."

Science describes joy as a buffer, a regulator, and a builder of resilience. In frequency justice, joy is all of these—and more. Each moment of joy you allow is a crystalline strike against distortion. It creates coherence that no amount of fear can unravel.

Joy does not ignore suffering. It shines within it. It says: we are still alive, and we will not stop imagining a better world. That imagination is the seedbed of liberation.

Joy is not escapism—it is resistance. Each laugh, each song, each shared moment of delight is a radical act of coherence in a fractured world.

CHAPTER 4

"Darkness cannot drive out darkness: only light can do that. Hate cannot drive out hate: only love can do that."

Dr. Martin Luther King Jr.

Chapter 5

The Role of Distortion & Transmutation

To understand frequency justice, we must also understand its opposite. If compassion, safety, and joy are the seeds of coherence, then distortion is the soil of disconnection. Distortion shows up as fear, greed, hatred, and despair. It convinces us that separation is real and that survival requires domination.

It is tempting to see distortion as evil. But distortion is more like static on a radio: interference that scrambles the signal of Source. It is real in its effects, but not ultimate in its power. Naming distortion clearly matters but inflating it only gives it more ground.

How Distortion Operates

Distortion spreads most effectively through:

- Fear loops in the nervous system. When we feel unsafe, distortion amplifies.

- Shame and isolation. When we believe we are broken, we disconnect from others and from Source.

- Oppressive systems. Distortion embeds itself in laws, policies, and cultures that benefit from keeping people afraid and divided.

Distortion is sticky—it tries to convince us that it is perma-nent. But nothing distorted can last.

The Power of Transmutation

Transmutation is the alchemy of turning density into light or distortion into coherence. It is not denial. It is not bypassing. It is the steady choice to bring compassion, safety, and joy directly into contact with distortion until the static clears.

Transmutation is the core mechanism of Frequency Justice: the process by which pain becomes information, infor-mation becomes clarity, and clarity becomes empowered choice. It is the engine that turns pain into power.

Rather than suppressing or bypassing difficult emotions, transmutation invites us to meet them directly—within a regulated nervous system—so that their inner intelligence can surface. Heart-level alchemy happens when you stay present instead of collapsing or numbing.

Pain is not inherently destructive; it is unrefined signal. When engaged consciously, it reveals what needs protec-tion, what requires witnessing, and what calls for change. In this framework, pain is not a flaw in the system but a messenger carrying instructions for coherence.

Pain softens when you stop running from it and instead ask: "What do you need from me?"

The heart can turn anything into medicine when you meet it gently.

Transmutation is impossible in a dysregulated system. This is the somatic truth: Until the nervous system shifts out of threat mode, pain cannot be processed. It loops. It overwhelms. It suffocates. Regulation is the doorway. Once you are safe inside your own body, emotion becomes digestible— and then transmutation begins.

Transmutation is ultimately practical:

- You feel

- You understand

- You decide

- You act

- You integrate

This is the transformation from suffering to sovereignty. Your pain becomes direction. Your direction becomes agency. Your agency becomes identity.

The ultimate role of transmutation is to restore inner sovereignty. Pain fragments the field—it scatters attention, distorts perception, and pulls us into old survival loops. Transmutation reorganizes the field by metabolizing emotional experience into meaning and direction.

This is the foundation of Frequency Justice: the recognition that every emotional state holds a form of relational or internal wisdom. Grief shows what mattered. Anger reveals where boundaries are needed. Fear signals unmet safety needs. Shame shows where identity and integrity have become misaligned. When these messages are understood rather than avoided, the system re-stabilizes.

Practice of Transmutation

Transmutation unfolds in a clear sequence:

1. Recognition	Naming the emotion moves it out of reactivity.
2. Regulation	Calming the nervous system so the signal becomes processable.
3. Receptivity	Turning toward the emotion and asking what it is trying to show.
4. Revelation	Identifying the truth or instruction hidden inside the pain.
5. Choice	Taking an action aligned with that truth.
6. Integration	Embodying the insight through ongoing behavior, boundaries, or identity shifts.

These steps convert raw emotional energy into agency and coherence, allowing the individual to reclaim their internal authority.

Within the Frequency Justice framework, transmutation is both personal and collective. Individually, it helps us identify where our field is collapsing and how to reorganize it around wisdom rather than fear. Collectively, it teaches that restoring coherence requires metabolizing anger, grief, and fragmentation into clarity, accountability, repair, and transformation. Justice is not only an external structure—it is an internal process that begins with the willingness to meet our own discomfort without abandoning ourselves. When pain is transmuted, the system becomes stronger, clearer, and more ethical.

This is why transmutation is described as the "engine" of Frequency Justice. It turns suffering into sovereignty, fragmentation into coherence, and emotional overwhelm into grounded power. It is the alchemical heart of the entire model—the process by which humans reclaim their agency and reorient their lives toward truth, clarity, and liberation.

Compassionate Reflection

- Where do I feel distortion most in my daily life?

- Which emotions are most challenging for me to transmute?

- Practice the steps of transmutation with a difficult emotion you are currently experiencing and journal below.

CHAPTER 5

"When we try to pick out anything by itself, we find it hitched to everything else in the Universe".

John Muir

Chapter 6

Nodes, Lattice, and Coherence

If compassion, safety, and joy are the choices of frequency justice, then nodes are their legacy. Every time you embody one of these frequencies, you create an imprint that does not fade when the moment ends. That imprint stabilizes the collective field, like a stone dropped into water sending ripples long after it sinks.

When enough imprints gather, they crystallize into nodes. And when nodes connect, they form the lattice—the living architecture of coherence that surrounds and sustains us all.

What Are Nodes?

A node is a point of stabilized frequency. It can be as small as the feeling of safety you create for a child in your home, or as large as the peace generated by a community singing together. Nodes are built through repetition, sincerity, and presence.

- A moment of compassion builds a compassion node.

- A safe conversation builds a safety node.

- A burst of shared laughter builds a joy node.

Some nodes dissolve quickly, like sparks in the dark. Others solidify and remain, accessible to anyone who passes through that space or remembers that moment.

The Lattice: Collective Memory of Humanity

The lattice is the interconnected web of nodes. It is humanity's frequency memory—a record of compassion, safety, and joy that weaves through time and space. The lattice is what allows people to feel unexpectedly calm in a sacred place, even if they have never been there before. It is what carries ancestral resilience forward through generations.

Distortion also creates imprints—fear, cruelty, despair—but those threads eventually unravel. Coherence endures. That is why the lattice of compassion and safety is stronger than the noise of distortion.

Coherence Defined

Coherence is the vibration of Source itself. It is the state of alignment where everything flows without distortion. In the body, coherence feels like breath that moves freely, heart rhythms that steady, and nervous systems that regulate. In the spirit, coherence feels like clarity, ease, and trust.

When we act in coherence, our individual pulse harmonizes with the larger field. This is why even small acts of compassion ripple wider than we imagine. They carry the vibration of Source, and Source never loses signal.

How You Build Nodes

You do not need to master metaphysics to build nodes. You are already doing it. Every time you return to compassion, even when you're afraid, you create one. Every time you soothe your nervous system instead of lashing out, you create another.

The difference is intention.

*   Unconscious acts of kindness create sparks.

*   Conscious, repeated acts create structures that endure.

By choosing compassion, safety, and joy deliberately, you are planting crystalline seeds that strengthen the lattice for generations.

A Living Example

Think of someone who has comforted you during your darkest hour. Their presence created safety that still lives in your memory. Even now, recalling it brings calm to your body. That memory is a node. It lives in the lattice, accessible again and again.

In the same way, the compassion you offer others may outlive the moment. They may carry it forward into their lives, offering safety and joy to others in your name.

Compassionate Reflection & Practice

Planting a Node

1. Choose one act of compassion, safety, or joy you can embody today.

   ○ Offer a kind word to yourself.

   ○ Make your home feel safe for a pet or loved one.

   ○ Allow yourself to laugh fully, without apology.

2. Pause as you do it. Whisper:

   "This moment plants a node of coherence. May it ripple outward."

3. Trust that the lattice receives it.

Closing

You are not separate from the lattice—you are one of its builders. Each node you create is a thread in the architecture of liberation. And as more of us commit to building nodes, the lattice of coherence grows stronger, until distortion has fewer places to hide.

Frequency justice is not only about today's choices—it is about the legacy those choices leave in the collective field. Your nodes will outlast you. That is how liberation becomes possible.

CHAPTER 6

"Small acts, when multiplied by millions of people, can transform the world".

Howard Zinn

Chapter 7

Living Frequency Justice

Frequency justice is not an idea to admire from a distance. It is a way of living—moment by moment, choice by choice. The lattice may be vast, nodes may sound mysterious, but the truth is simple: frequency justice is lived in the ordinary.

It is in the words we speak to ourselves.

It is in how we greet our neighbors.

It is in how we pause before reacting to fear.

Living frequency justice means letting compassion, safety, and joy infuse the fabric of daily life.

In Daily Life

- Compassion: Instead of berating yourself for being tired, whisper: "Of course I'm tired. May I rest."

- Safety: Instead of scrolling endlessly when anxious, step outside, feel your feet on the earth, and remind your body: "I belong here."

- Joy: Instead of saving delight for rare occasions, notice the small glimmers—a bird's song, a sip of warm tea, a moment of laughter.

These choices may not look radical from the outside, but inside the lattice, they are revolutions.

In Relationships

Frequency justice is contagious. The way you hold your frequency shifts others.

- Offering compassion to a friend rather than judgment creates space for healing.

- Setting clear, kind boundaries builds relational safety.

- Bringing humor or play into a tense situation restores balance.

In this way, you become a stabilizer for those around you—not by force, but by resonance.

In Community

When practiced collectively, frequency justice builds resilient communities.

- A group that values compassion will not collapse into cruelty when stressed.

- A workplace that centers safety will weather conflict with integrity.

- A movement that prioritizes joy will endure longer than one fueled by anger alone.

Living frequency justice together turns ordinary spaces into nodes of coherence.

The Humble Hero

You do not need a platform or recognition to live frequency justice. You do not need to call yourself an activist or a healer. Living frequency justice is heroic precisely because it is humble.

- The mother who calms her child with tenderness.

- The neighbor who checks in on the elderly man next door.

- The worker who quietly refuses to spread gossip.

These acts may never be recorded in history books, but they build the lattice more powerfully than speeches or slogans.

Compassionate Reflection & Practice

1. Where in my daily life can I choose compassion instead of criticism?

2. How can I create safety for myself and others today?

3. What small joy can I allow without apology?

Try this: Before bed tonight, review your day. Name one act of compassion, one act of safety, and one act of joy. Whisper gratitude for each. Trust that they joined the lattice.

Closing

Living frequency justice is not about perfection. It is about returning—again and again—to the frequencies that heal. Each return is enough. Each act matters.

You are already living it. This chapter is your reminder to notice it, trust it, and amplify it.

"Nobody's free until everybody's free"

Fannie Lou Hamer

Chapter 8

Toward Collective Liberation

Frequency justice begins as personal practice—how we speak to ourselves, how we regulate our nervous systems, how we choose compassion, safety, and joy in the smallest of moments. But its true purpose is collective. Liberation is never just for one person; it is always for all.

Every act of frequency justice ripples outward. Every node you plant strengthens the lattice for your family, your community, your city, your planet and your timeline. The lattice does not ask who you are, what you believe, or whether you feel worthy. It simply carries the frequencies you place within it.

Liberation as More Than Absence of Harm

We often think of liberation as the end of oppression, the dismantling of harmful systems. That matters deeply—but liberation is not only the absence of harm. It is the presence of flourishing.

- Liberation is children growing up with safety in their bodies.

- Liberation is communities organizing around joy instead of fear.

- Liberation is compassion woven into policy, art, and culture.

- Liberation is the freedom to create, to rest, to dream, without fear.

Frequency justice plants the seeds of this flourishing world.

The World in Coherence

Imagine what would happen if compassion, safety, and joy were the dominant vibrations of our time.

- Families would carry less generational trauma.

- Neighborhoods would feel less fractured.

- Movements for justice would be steadier, harder to break.

- Systems could be rebuilt not on control, but on care.

This is not fantasy. It is coherence—what the lattice remembers is possible when enough people choose to live differently.

You Are Already Part of This

You may feel small in the face of oppression. You may wonder if your single choice to soften your breath or smile at a stranger could ever matter. But remember: nodes accumulate. The lattice magnifies what you contribute.

Your part is not to fix everything. Your part is to choose, again and again, to return to compassion, safety, and joy. That return is enough. That return is powerful.

Compassionate Reflection & Practice

Envisioning Liberation

1. Close your eyes. Imagine the lattice of the world glowing brighter, node by node.

2. See compassion spreading through conversations, safety in homes, joy in communities.

3. Whisper: "May my life be a seed of liberation."

4. Trust that your vision strengthens the collective field.

Closing

Frequency justice is not a destination. It is a way of walking. It is how we keep moving through distortion without becoming it. It is how we plant seeds for futures we may never see, but that our children will inherit.

You are already part of this weaving. You have always been. Each choice you make is another thread in the tapestry of liberation. And together, our threads become a world reborn.

"Change your frequency. Change the world".

Nikola Tesla

Chapter 9

Envisioning a World Woven in Frequency
Justice

A Future Rooted in Compassion

Imagine communities where compassion is no longer
optional, but the baseline of how systems function. In
healthcare, policies are built on listening, empathy, and
equitable access. In education, children are seen not as
empty vessels to be filled but as luminous beings to be
nurtured. Compassion is not a private virtue but a struc-
tural one—woven into laws, workplaces, and relationships.

Safety as the Nervous System of Society

When societies embody safety, the nervous system of the
collective shifts. Crime lessens not through punishment, but
through prevention, belonging, and healing. Homes and
neighborhoods become sanctuaries. People feel safe to be
themselves, to walk freely, to love openly. Safety is no longer
reactive but proactive—a lattice that steadies the whole.

Joy as the Revolutionary Act

Joy becomes not frivolous, but essential. Parks, art, music, and celebration are prioritized as much as roads and commerce. Joy reclaims its place as a measure of prosperity. A joyful society resists distortion because joy vibrates at a frequency distortion cannot penetrate. In joy, people remember they are free.

A Collective Lattice of Liberation

When compassion, safety, and joy become the scaffolding of systems, the crystalline lattice stabilizes. Distortion cannot take root where coherence is strong. Each person becomes a node—a point of light adding to the collective grid of liberation. Together, they weave a living architecture of Source on Earth.

Compassionate Reflection

- How can I embody compassion in one concrete way today?

- Where can I create safety for myself and others?

- What small act of joy can ripple outward into the lattice?

This vision is not fantasy—it is already beginning. Every moment you choose compassion over indifference, safety over fear, joy over despair, you weave another thread of frequency justice into the eternal fabric. The future is built not in grand gestures, but in countless quiet choices aligned with coherence.

CHAPTER 9

"The old world is dying, and the new world struggles to be born. Now is the time of monsters."

Antonio Gramsci

Chapter 10

The Great Unraveling: Living Through Difficult Times

We are living through an unraveling. Systems built on fear, domination, and distortion are crumbling under their own weight. It is easy to feel despair, to mistake collapse for the end. But collapse is also opening. In the space where distortion falls away, a lattice of compassion, safety, and joy can take root.

This is where Frequency Justice lives.

Each act of compassion, each moment of safety, each spark of joy is not small. It is a node in the crystalline lattice, holding the planet steady as distortion shakes loose. You may feel ordinary, average, or even inadequate at times. Yet your presence, your coherence, your willingness to choose love in the face of fear—these alter the vibration of the whole.

This work is not only for today. What you plant now will ripple forward for generations. Children yet unborn will benefit from the seeds of coherence you scatter. They will still know struggle, but because of what you and others choose now, they will also inherit tools, language, and resonance that make freedom easier to claim.

The world will heal through millions of steady flames choosing compassion over cruelty, safety over fear, joy over despair. This is revolutionary work. It is liberation work. And it is work that you, reader, are fully capable of.

May this book serve as a reminder: you are not powerless in the face of distortion. You are part of the flame that makes coherence possible. Together, our resonance will outlast the collapse and seed the future.

Afterword

A Blessing for the Journey

If you've read this far, know this: you are already a participant in frequency justice. You always have been. Every time you chose compassion when anger was easier, every time you created safety for another being, every time you allowed joy to rise in your chest—you were part of this great weaving.

This book is not a set of instructions to follow perfectly. It is a mirror, reminding you of what you already carry. You have always known how to build coherence. You have always known how to return to love, even after fear.

I don't know what your path looks like from here. You may take bold steps into new ways of living, or you may continue with the same rhythm, sprinkling small acts of compassion into your days. Both are sacred. Both matter.

The truth is, we will never fully see the impact of our choices. We will not always know which seeds take root or how far the ripples travel. But the lattice remembers. The lattice holds. And your thread is woven in.

So as you close this book, I offer you this blessing:

May you feel safe enough to rest and be at ease.

May you feel compassion flowing through you and to you.

May you laugh often and let joy be your strength.

May your life be a seed of liberation, and may you trust that it is enough.

May we all be free.

With gratitude and infinite love,

Nickie Sloan

Definitions

The Spiritual Language of Frequency Justice

The language I use throughout this book draws from several disciplines that all describe patterns, structures, and interactions in different ways. In physics and quantum models, we see lattice-structures and nodal points used to map networks, interactions, and fields. I draw from that language because I perceive analogous structures in the human relational and spiritual field—energetic nodes of interaction, and a lattice of connection and coherence that shapes how we affect one another.

My usage of these terms is not identical to their scientific definitions, nor is it limited to metaphor. It sits in the middle—what I consider a metaphor-to-experience bridge. Quantum language provides an accessible model, while my clinical work, contemplative practice, and lived spiritual experience suggest that similar patterns may exist in the subtle emotional and energetic architecture of human connection.

These definitions are offered to support clarity, grounding, and transparency. Readers are invited to engage with them according to their own worldview—whether symbolic, metaphysical, experiential, or simply as conceptual tools for understanding how humans influence, regulate, and transform one another.

Coherence

Physics Definition:

In wave mechanics, optics, and quantum theory, coherence is the degree of phase alignment or synchronized behavior between waves or quantum states. High coherence produces clear patterns; low coherence results in noise or interference.

Metaphysical / Spiritual Definition:

A felt sense of inner harmony, alignment, and resonance—emotionally, energetically, or spiritually. Coherence reflects clarity, groundedness, and regulated presence.

Frequency Justice Usage:

Coherence refers to the emotional-spiritual alignment that supports regulation, compassion, connection, and healing.

Crystalline

Physics Definition:

In physics and materials science, crystalline describes solids whose atoms or molecules are arranged in highly ordered, repeating lattice structures. These structures have stability, symmetry, and consistent vibrational properties.

Metaphysical / Spiritual Definition:

A state of refined, high-frequency clarity and aligned energetic structure. "Crystalline" often symbolizes purity, insight, and elevated consciousness.

Frequency Justice Usage:

Crystalline refers to a clear, stable, and coherent state within the human energetic-emotional field—where healing, compassion, and regulation can be transmitted cleanly.

Distortion

Physics Definition:

In physics and engineering, distortion refers to changes or deviations in a signal, wave, or structure—alterations that disrupt the integrity or expected pattern.

Metaphysical / Spiritual Definition:

A disruption or misalignment in emotional, energetic, or spiritual flow. Distortion reflects fragmentation, fear, unresolved trauma, or energetic interference.

Frequency Justice Usage:

Distortion describes emotional or energetic patterns that interrupt coherence, connection, or healing—often arising from dysregulation or unprocessed experience.

Frequency Justice

Frequency justice is the living principle that compassion, safety, and joy are coherent frequencies that resist distortion and restore balance. Frequency Justice is a practical map for restoring coherence in the individual and planetary field.

Grid

Physics Definition:

A grid is an ordered arrangement of points used for measurement, mapping, or simulation in physics. Grids help represent fields, forces, and interactions within space.

Metaphysical / Spiritual Definition:

A network or energetic framework through which spiritual, emotional, or collective energy organizes, moves, or is distributed.

Frequency Justice Usage:

A grid refers to the larger pattern of relational and energetic interconnectedness—an organizing framework within which nodes, lattices, and coherence function.

Lattice

Physics Definition:

A lattice is a structured, often repeating pattern of points in space used to model physical systems such as crystals, quantum fields, and atomic interactions.

Metaphysical / Spiritual Definition:

A subtle network or pattern of energetic connection that reflects how humans relate, resonate, and influence one another on emotional or spiritual levels.

Frequency Justice Usage:

A lattice represents the subtle architecture of human connection as I perceive it—an energetic-relational structure underlying healing and resonance.

Node

Physics Definition:

In physics, a node is a point where interactions meet or where certain physical quantities (like wave amplitude) reach zero. Nodes appear in quantum wavefunctions, lattice structures, and network theory.

Metaphysical / Spiritual Definition:

A point of concentrated emotional, energetic, or relational significance where connection, intuition, or healing is heightened.

Frequency Justice Usage:

A node is a point of relational or energetic intensity within the human emotional-spiritual field—where connection, insight, or influence gathers.

About the Author

 **Nichole Sloan (Nickie)** is a licensed clinical social worker, trauma-informed therapist, and longtime practitioner of mindfulness and compassion-based healing. For over two decades, she has walked alongside others in their journeys toward wholeness, weaving together deep listening, emotional attunement, and somatic presence to create spaces where transformation can unfold.

With a background in both clinical mental health and contemplative practices, Nickie's work bridges science and soul. She is a devoted advocate for nervous system healing, vibrational awareness, and the reclamation of inner sovereignty. Her writings and teachings explore the intersection of emotional resilience, energetic integrity, and collective liberation.

Nickie lives in Georgia, where she tends to her garden, cares for animals and listens deeply to the rhythms of nature. She enjoys traveling, creating art, contemplative practices and engaging in community care and advocacy. She believes that healing is not a destination but a remembering of one's own wisdom and power.